Compassion

RESOURCES FOR BIBLICAL LIVING

Lou Priolo, series editor

Compassion

Seeing with Jesus' Eyes

JOSHUA MACK

PUBLISHING
P.O. BOX 817 • PHILLIPSBURG • NEW JERSEY 08865-0817

Unless otherwise indicated, Scripture quotations are from the ESV® Bible (The Holy Bible, English Standard Version®), copyright © 2001 by Crossway, a publishing ministry of Good News Publishers. Used by permission. All rights reserved.

Scripture quotation marked (NASB) is from the *NEW AMERICAN STANDARD BIBLE*®. ©Copyright The Lockman Foundation 1960, 1962, 1963, 1968, 1971, 1972, 1973, 1975, 1977. Used by permission.

Italics within Scripture quotations indicate emphasis added.

ISBN: 978-1-62995-069-3 (pbk)
ISBN: 978-1-62995-070-9 (ePub)
ISBN: 978-1-62995-071-6 (Mobi)

Printed in the United States of America

Library of Congress Cataloging-in-Publication Data

Mack, Joshua.
 Compassion : seeing with Jesus' eyes / Joshua Mack.
     pages cm. -- (Resources for biblical living)
 Includes bibliographical references.
 ISBN 978-1-62995-069-3 (pbk.) -- ISBN 978-1-62995-070-9 (epub) --
ISBN 978-1-62995-071-6 (mobi)
 1. Compassion--Religious aspects--Christianity. I. Title.
 BV4647.S9M33 2015
 241'.4--dc23
                        2015020353

IT IS NICE to be right.

Who doesn't like winning Trivial Pursuit or knowing the answer to a question that many others do not?

There are times when being right is not only nice, but important. You can't afford to be wrong about God, about salvation, about Jesus Christ, about the Scriptures, about the Christian life. When being wrong has consequences like possibly going to hell, you know that being right matters.

Some people become so focused on the importance of being right, however, they begin to act as if being right is *all* that matters. It is as if they think that as long as they are right in what they are saying, then they are right altogether.

But they are wrong.

There's More to Being Right Than Being Right

Not only is it important to be right about truth, it's also important to feel right toward people.

Underline the word *feel*.

How you feel about other people is absolutely, vitally important. God wants you to be emotionally invested in people to the point where you sincerely rejoice when they rejoice and weep when they weep (see Rom. 12:15), where their interests become yours (see Phil. 2:1–4), where your heart is soft toward them and they know it (see Matt. 18:27). The Bible calls this deep concern for people *compassion*. Without compassion, no matter how right you are in what you are saying, you are wrong in how you are acting.

One proof that this is true is the fact that God commands us to be compassionate.

In Colossians 3, Paul explains the difference the gospel should make in the way we, as believers, treat people. After telling us to put away things like anger, wrath, malice, slander, and obscene talk, he goes on to tell us as God's chosen ones, holy and beloved, to put on compassionate hearts. The word Paul uses for *compassion* has to do with feelings of sympathy, and he says we are to have these feelings of sympathy for other people deep down in the innermost parts of our hearts. As people who have been shown such compassion—to be chosen! to be set apart! to be loved by God!—we should be clothed in compassion ourselves, as one of the distinguishing characteristics of our new lives as followers of Christ.

It is not only the direct commands to be compassionate that highlight the importance of compassion, however. It is also all the commands Scripture gives us to love others. Whenever you read a call to love in the Bible, you are reading a command that in one way or another requires you to be compassionate. Loving people is more than being interested in their good and having certain feelings toward them, but it is certainly not less. How can anyone think he loves someone else if he merely says the right things to her and does the right things for her, without actually caring for her? That's not called love; that's called pretending.

And biblical love is much bigger and better than that.

Here is how Peter puts it. "Having purified your souls by your obedience to the truth for a sincere brotherly love, love one another earnestly from a pure heart" (1 Peter 1:22). One of the reasons God saved you was to enable you to love other people in a way that is real.

There are lots of important terms in this particular passage that describe the kind of love you are to have for others. And each of them calls for something to be going on in your heart.

Take for example the word *brotherly*. Peter is talking to you as a believer, and he is saying you are to love others *like family*.

This means that the relationships you have with others are to be way beyond merely casual ones. Imagine saying that you love someone like a brother but then not hurting when he hurts. Brotherly love requires compassion.

Another term Peter uses in verse 22 to describe the way you ought to love others is found in the command itself: "Love one another." The term that is translated *love* comes from the familiar Greek word *agape*. The greatest example of agape is the sacrificial example of Jesus Christ. He loved you by going to the cross in your place. Is it possible to love people like that without intensely wanting their best? Of course not! Loving others like Jesus loved you is going to require more sacrifice than simply being interested in their good, but still, it is going to require at least that. Agape love assumes compassion.

Learning to love others better is something you need to take seriously. I think that's what Peter is getting at when he uses the term *earnestly*. *Earnestly* is a word that indicates commitment and zeal. This verse could even be translated, "Love one another strainingly." Peter wants believers to flat-out *work* at loving others. You are to make a priority of pursuing something far beyond casual relationships with others, of working hard at developing family-like relationships, of making a habit of sacrificing for other people's good, of thinking about ways in which you can express Christlike love to others, and of being bothered and concerned when you don't.

And, most importantly, you are to do all this from the heart.

This heartfelt love may be where Peter actually places his greatest emphasis. Notice how he repeats himself. "Having purified your souls by your obedience to the truth for a *sincere* brotherly love, love one another earnestly from *a pure* heart." This means it is not enough to say the right thing or even do the right thing; you need to work at feeling the right thing. Sincere love requires compassion. If you are going to be the kind of person God wants you to be, who He saved you to be, you need to do more than just look like you care for the people you are speaking to; you need to actually care—and if you don't, you need to make a priority out of becoming a person who does.[1]

The kind of love the Bible demands, demands that. And the fact is, it demands it a lot.

God puts all kinds of different exclamation points throughout Scripture to highlight the importance of love. It is how the world will know that you are one of Jesus' disciples (see John 13:33–35). It is described as the greatest commandment in the law of God (Matt. 22:37–40). We are told that great spiritual gifts plus great faith plus great sacrifice minus love equals nothing (1 Cor. 13:1–3). Can you think of any other command in Scripture that is emphasized more? Perhaps it might help if God prefaced one of the commands to love with a phrase like *above all*. Oh, wait. He did. Twice. "And *above all these* put on love, which binds everything together in perfect harmony" (Col. 3:14). "*Above all*, keep loving one another earnestly, since love covers a multitude of sins" (1 Peter 4:8).

It is strange for someone to claim to love the Bible without taking seriously what the Bible says about love. But it happens all too often. Certainly, there are people who minimize the importance of truth. But there are also many who minimize the importance of caring about people. And sometimes the very people who say they are most serious about truth seem to be the least serious about the truths that the Bible teaches about showing compassion to others.

This doesn't make sense.

It is impossible to love people without loving truth. Love without truth is no love at all. But it is equally impossible to disconnect a sincere love for truth from a deep love for people. We should not try to serve people without a love for God. We must not try to serve God without a love for people.

1. The command to be compassionate and the commands to love are, in part, commands to feel. They, like all scriptural commands, are something that true believers can learn to do by God's enabling power.

8

Passion for Truth Must Produce Compassion for People

There are several reasons why this is so. The first is practical. The person who sincerely loves truth wants others to love it too. Truth is valuable, and people who love it know that others desperately need it. It is hard to understand how anyone who has been impacted by the truth would ever want to get in the way of someone else being changed by it. But that's what you and I do when we are passionate about the truth without being compassionate toward people.

Lack of compassion makes the truth look ugly. For those who are familiar with truth, that may hardly seem possible. It is a little like standing at the edge of the Grand Canyon for the first time and having our guide tell us that someone could make that scene look ugly. But it's possible! I guarantee that if someone pushes you over the edge, the Grand Canyon is not going to look nearly as beautiful to you on the way down as it did while you were standing there gazing at it. It is possible for you to make something that's as beautiful as truth seem ugly to others if your passion for it isn't combined with compassion for them.[2]

One reason a lack of compassion makes the truth look so ugly is that people quickly realize it is a sham. Not the truth, but instead the person's supposed passion for it. John puts it like this: "If anyone says, 'I love God,' and hates his brother, he is a liar; for he who does not love his brother whom he has seen cannot love God whom he has not seen" (1 John 4:20). A failure to love people is a failure to love God. Those who say they love God, but who don't love people, are lying.

2. This does not mean that you will never speak earnestly, boldly, or even sharply to others. Compassion sometimes requires that. When you see someone about to push someone else off the Grand Canyon, for example, it would not be compassionate to speak nonchalantly, as if nothing urgent were at stake. In our contemporary culture, this reality is very important to understand. We are constantly being pressured to think that anytime we speak in a way that may appear negative to anyone we are being unloving. But this is not true. Biblical compassion is greater than simply being polite.

Those Who Know God Best Also Love People Most

Every time we see someone in Scripture who loved God, we also see that person loving people.

Paul is a great example of that. You don't get much deeper than the apostle Paul. This was a theologian's theologian. He was a man who loved truth. And yet when you read Paul's letters you see very quickly that he was also a man who cared deeply for people and who let them know it.

I actually get a little embarrassed sometimes by the way Paul speaks to people. Take what he tells the Philippians:

> It is right for me to feel this way about you all, because *I hold you in my heart*, for you are all partakers with me of grace, both in my imprisonment and in the defense and confirmation of the gospel. For God is my witness, how *I yearn for you all* with *the affection* of Christ Jesus. (Phil. 1:7–8)

Now *yearn* is a pretty intense word. I can't imagine using it to describe my feelings for anyone other than God and my wife. Yet Paul did.

And this deep affection for people impacted the way in which Paul ministered to them. He didn't keep his feelings hidden away in his heart. He let them spill out all over the people he was serving. He says to the Thessalonians,

> But we were gentle among you, *like a nursing mother taking care of her own children*. So, being *affectionately desirous* of you, we were ready to share with you not only the gospel of God but also our own selves, because *you had become very dear to us.* (1 Thess. 2:7–9)

It is not every man's way of relating to people that can be compared to a nursing mother. In fact, if you compared most men to a nursing mother they might take it as an insult. But not Paul.

He was happy to remind the Thessalonians how his love for them produced such gentle and tender care. Paul was not afraid to let people know that he loved them.

While some people may have questions about some of the things that he wrote, there is no one who could objectively question his passion for truth and his compassion for people. Reading Paul's letters, you never wonder what he feels about the gospel and you never wonder what he feels about people. In fact, if you want an encouraging exercise, you might just work your way through one of Paul's letters and underline all the different ways he expresses his love and concern for the people to whom he's writing. It's stunning! How many different ways can one man find to say he is *for* someone?

There is only one person in Scripture I can think of who is a better example than Paul is of how inextricably connected love for truth and love for people should be, and that is *Jesus Himself.* I don't think I need to convince you of Jesus' passion for truth, given the fact that He is the truth (see John 14:6). But perhaps I can remind you of Jesus' deep compassion for people. As B. B. Warfield once said,

> The emotion which we should naturally expect to find most frequently attributed to that Jesus whose whole life was a mission of mercy, and whose ministry was so marked by deeds of beneficence that it was summed up in the memory of his followers as a going through the land "doing good" (Acts 9:36), is no doubt compassion. In point of fact, this is the emotion which is most frequently attributed to him.[3]

If you ever doubt Jesus' compassion for people, you should spend some time reading the Gospels. What you will find time and time again throughout the Gospels is that Jesus saw, Jesus felt, and Jesus acted. In fact, as Charles Spurgeon

3. Benjamin B. Warfield, *The Person and Work of Christ* (Philadelphia: Presbyterian and Reformed Publishing, 1980), 97.

once said, "If you want to summarize the whole character of Christ in reference to ourselves, it might be gathered into this one sentence, 'He was moved with compassion.' "[4] God sent something a whole lot better than a set of mp3s or YouTube videos when He sent His Son into this world. He sent a person who loved the people to whom He was ministering so much that He entered into their world, felt their pain, was moved emotionally by their problems, preached the truth to them, and gave Himself up for their good. Jesus loved the truth and loved people, and if you are going to serve Him, you need to do the same.

If you claim to be passionate about the truth, you need to look long and hard at the one who is Truth, Jesus. You need to see the Creator becoming a servant on the very earth He created. You need to watch as He serves not only His glorious Father but also His unworthy creatures. You need to listen as He speaks to them *and weeps with them.* Is there any limit to Christ's self-sacrificing love? Notice how far His love for people took Him—all the way to dying on a cross! Can anyone think of anything more shocking than this? How wonderful it is that the dearly loved Son of God would care so deeply for the stubborn, rebellious enemies of God that He would gladly choose to bear the wrath of God so that these enemies could enter into fellowship with God as dearly loved children, too!

You need to see Jesus like this, because Jesus like this is your example. "Be imitators of me," Paul says, "as I am of Christ" (1 Cor. 11:1). You serve a Savior whose heart was broken by the needs of people and whose body was broken for their good. And something is broken in your heart if you say you are passionate about the truth while being uncompassionate toward people.[5]

4. Charles Spurgeon, "The Compassion of Jesus" (sermon no. 3438, Metropolitan Tabernacle, Newington, London), available online at The Spurgeon Archive, accessed November 1, 2013, http://www.spurgeon.org/sermons/3438.htm.
5. "If then we think we are approved by God and love does not reign in us, we deceive ourselves. The world may applaud us, but our whole life will be utterly loathsome, until love is established in our hearts, so that she governs, and we tend always to that end, yes,

Where Compassion Begins

I sometimes tell people I have learned a lot about God from a boy who can't talk.

One of our foster sons had a stroke in his mother's womb, and as a result he has a difficult time talking, walking—really a difficult time doing much else besides smiling. He does a lot of that.

I was thinking about him recently as I was studying Ephesians 1:3–5, where Paul tells us that in love God predestined us to be adopted as sons. There is so much in this passage to enjoy. In love, before the beginning of the world, God chose us to be part of His family, with all the rights and privileges of real sons. But I guess what stood out to me more than ever before was the fact that I don't bring anything to the table but sin. It is not as though God adopted children into His family because He was needy, because He was up in heaven always wishing to have a child, because these children would be intelligent conversation partners, because they were sweet and innocent. No, all that these children whom God decided to adopt had—all I had—was sin. And what's more, it's not just that the adoption itself is a gift, it is that anything good we bring to God now as His children is a gift as well! Our worship, our gratitude, our praises—all these are gifts that God purchased for us at a cost.

And wow, think about the cost!

He adopted children like us at the cost of His own perfect Son, with whom He had an absolutely perfect relationship already. What kindness! It is a joy to be able to be a slave of

and perform all our works by her. Now then, seeing that love is the true perfection of the faithful and of God's children, let us see what it consists of. For if a man boasts that he has it, and in the meanwhile has neither lowliness, nor gentleness, nor patience, he makes the Holy Spirit a liar, who not without reason shows what is signified by charity or love. For he has not set down the bare word and simply said, be loving, but he has also shown us what is meant by it" (John Calvin, *Sermons on Ephesians* [Carlisle, PA: The Banner of Truth Trust, 1973], 323).

God—but we are not just slaves, we are sons and daughters, and not because we will ever get to the point where we have something that God needs. It's all grace! It's all compassion!

I am convinced that becoming more compassionate toward others begins with enjoying God's compassion toward oneself.

Compassion begins with worship.

A Compassion Problem Is a Worship Problem

I know what it's like to defend yourself and to come up with excuses for your lack of compassion. I am pretty good at doing it myself. You might blame your temperament, or you could talk about the family in which you were raised. I have known people who would even try to make their lack of compassion sound holy by saying they were just more concerned about truth than most other people were. But ultimately a lack of compassion is not simply a "personality" problem or a "people" problem.

A lack of compassion is a worship problem.

Jesus made that clear. Listen to the way He rebukes the Pharisees. "If you had known what this means, 'I desire compassion and not sacrifice,' you would not have condemned the guiltless" (Matt. 12:7).

Isn't that startling? It's jaw dropping. Of course God desired sacrifice. He's the one who instituted it. He's the one who gave very detailed instructions in the Bible about how it was to be done. So what does Jesus mean? He means that if anyone thinks he can truly worship God through external acts of worship *alone*, without a heart of compassion and mercy, he hasn't read his Bible closely enough.

The Pharisees' failure to show compassion was a big deal *because* it was a failure to worship God the way He wanted them to.[6]

6. For an extended treatment of this topic, see Jonathan Edwards's sermon "Mercy Not Sacrifice." It can be found in *The Works of Jonathan Edwards, vol. 22: Sermons and*

Sometimes people think of compassion as something that is important only for those who are "wired" that way. Worse, some people think of compassion as a subject that only women should be interested in. While it's true that some people may be more gifted in showing compassion than others, and that certainly one's "personality" may affect the way in which he demonstrates compassion, at the end of the day compassion is not so much about personality or giftedness or gender as it is about having a God-centered way of looking at the world.

There is no one more compassionate than God.

The psalmist tells us, "As a father shows compassion to his children, so the LORD shows compassion to those who fear him" (Ps. 103:13).

And as believers, we have experienced His great compassion in our salvation. We now come to Him as Father. We have access to the throne of grace. We know that His Son sympathizes with us in our weaknesses. We cast our cares upon Him, because we know He cares for us.

How is it possible to enjoy all these privileges solely as a result of God's compassionate kindness through Christ and His work on the cross without becoming more kind and compassionate ourselves?

It isn't.

You always become like what you worship.[7]

People who worship a compassionate God become compassionate themselves.

This is why I love talking about showing compassion to others. I know I will *first* have to talk about God and His compassion toward us as believers. This is how Paul motivated believers toward compassionate, forgiving love in Ephesians 4:32–5:2.

Discourses, 1739–1742, ed. Harry S. Stout and Nathan O. Hatch, with Kyle P. Farley (New Haven, CT: Yale University Press, 2003).

7. "Whatever people revere, they resemble, either for ruin or restoration" (G. K. Beale, *We Become What We Worship: A Biblical Theology of Idolatry* [Downers Grove, IL: IVP Academic, 2008], 16). Beale contends that the essence of the biblical conception of idolatry is that we take on the characteristics of what we worship.

He writes,

> Be kind to one another, tenderhearted, forgiving one another, as God in Christ forgave you. Therefore be imitators of God, as beloved children. And walk in love, as Christ loved us and gave himself up for us, a fragrant offering and sacrifice to God.

It is deep gratitude for being forgiven that produces love.

Paul is saying, "Because God in Christ has forgiven you, therefore you should seek to imitate God in your relationships with others by forgiving them and loving them sacrificially."

When you meet someone who has a hard time loving others in this way, you are meeting someone who doesn't fully appreciate the greatness of God's forgiveness. And when you meet someone who doesn't appreciate the greatness of God's forgiveness, you are meeting someone who doesn't fully appreciate the greatness of God.

It is that simple.

Jesus Himself puts it like this in Luke 7:47: "He who is forgiven little, loves little."

Now since there is no one who has been forgiven by God who has been forgiven little, Jesus has to be talking about a deep gratitude and appreciation for forgiveness. What He is saying is that the person who lacks a deep appreciation for forgiveness lacks love. If you want to grow in your love for God and others, then one place to start is to ask God to help you grow in your gratitude and thankfulness for how much He has forgiven you. And if you want to grow in your gratitude and thankfulness for how much He has forgiven you, you should also ask God to help you grow in your understanding of your own sinfulness.[8] A heart that is broken over its sin is a heart that will break for others.

This is why Paul calls our attention back to God and His gracious treatment of us as he challenges us to show forgiving

---

8. This could prove a painful proposition, but the painful recognition of your own sin may make it easier for you to feel the pain of others.

love. God's forgiveness of you and your love for others are tied together. If you want to become a genuine, sacrificially loving, and compassionate person, you will find motivation not by looking first and foremost at the people around you but instead by continually looking up to God as Father through Christ in worship.

It's good theology that drives biblical mercy.

I love how Paul puts it here in Ephesians 5:1: "Therefore be imitators of God."

I like that—because how do you imitate someone?

To imitate someone you have to watch him. You have to study him. You have to know him! It is wrong to talk about compassion as if it were somehow disconnected from our knowledge of God, because to love other people the way you ought, you have to know God so well that you understand how to imitate Him in the nitty-gritty issues of your daily life.

You will never have to love anyone who deserves your love less than you deserve the love of God. You will never have to forgive someone more than God has already forgiven you. You will never have to show more compassion to someone than God has already shown to you. That's why forgiveness and compassion and love toward others is such a test of how well you, as a believer, understand the gospel and are maturing in the knowledge of God. These are the kinds of attitudes and actions that reveal what you really believe and what you really understand about how holy God is, how sinful you are, and how much you need Jesus.

Before Your Heart Will Go Out toward People, Your Heart Must Go Up to God

When my wife and I moved to Africa to care for orphans, we had no idea what we were in for. We just knew that we wanted to show God's love to needy children. We had three girls of our own at the time, so we decided when we arrived that we would adopt only girls—that way we could keep the rooms pink and the Barbie collection growing. We had visited a particular HIV children's home several times, and my wife ended up phoning the director and asking whether she had any little girls in need of a family. She told us that she had a little girl whom they really needed to move because they had no more room, but that there was also a little boy who had come to their home the same day she had, and that he was really attached to her and was "such a fragile soul."

I don't remember our really discussing it, or thinking about it, or spending hours or days praying about it. I only remember our thinking, "A fragile soul? How can we say no to a fragile soul?" We painted a room blue and picked up a boy and a girl to bring home. We look back now and think how very crazy and God-ordained it was that we did not ask anything about these children beforehand. The only thing we knew was that they were HIV-positive and needed a home, and that Muzi was "a fragile soul."

A fragile soul he was. He was three years old when he came to our home. He was not potty trained, did not walk, did not talk, did not smile, did not laugh. He ate everything, including paper and sand and anything he saw lying on the floor in his reach, and we learned quickly that he would keep eating at any meal until we actually stopped him. If we set him on the floor, he would have been content to just sit there and not move all day, if we had let him. We would often comment to each other, "I wonder where he is?" It seemed sometimes as if there was no one home in that little body. He was deathly afraid of my coming in to hug him goodnight and would scream and crawl to the corner of his bed. He took his medications every twelve hours, and because of all these meds he had a continual runny tummy. Every morning, and every afternoon after his nap, we knew we would find him covered in diarrhea from head to toe, and so showers and washing bedding became a normal part of our day. Showers were "torture" to him, and so getting him cleaned up was a real battle, to say the least.

Over the years, we have learned a lot from having Muzi as part of our family. One of the big things we have learned about compassion is that it is hard. It is a lot easier to feel for someone when you do not have to clean him up every day. If you are going to show compassion for people over a long period of time, you need an even stronger motivation than simply the trouble they have found themselves in. No one could need compassion more than Muzi did, but our hearts are so sinful that, in the middle of the difficulties of caring for him, we could look at his need for help and, instead of feeling compassion, feel tired, selfish, and even annoyed.

Honestly, it is this way with pretty much anyone who is in trouble. From a distance you often feel sorry for such a person, but when you get in there and actually try to help, you will sometimes become discouraged by what you discover. When you focus your attention only on people, you can find all kinds of reasons not to feel much compassion for them or to reach out to them in love. It is when you are looking up to God the Father and His Son Jesus that all those reasons disappear.

Sanctification by Staring

Unfortunately, if there is one thing many people are slow to do in this modern world, it is to spend much time thinking about God or looking long and hard at Jesus. People like hearing about themselves, but Jesus, not so much—unless someone is talking about what Jesus can do for them. They want to hear sermons about being good people and how to have a successful life. That is one reason why there are all sorts of preaching about self and all kinds of talk about life in this world. But where is Jesus Christ?

This failure to focus on Jesus is a problem for many reasons. One reason it is a problem is because when people stop beholding

Jesus, they stop seeing others. Man-centered religious activity leads to "me-centered" living. The more you focus on your needs, the less you feel for the needs of others. We fight self-centered living through Christ-centered worship. Paul explains the process in 2 Corinthians 3:18: "And we all, with unveiled face, beholding the glory of the Lord, are being transformed into the same image from one degree of glory to another."

God makes us more like Christ as we look to Christ in faith as He is revealed to us in God's Word. In other words, it is as you behold Jesus and adore Him that you become like Him.

When you begin to see how big Jesus really is, you start to see how small you really are. When you start to see how small you are, you begin to appreciate how much Jesus stooped down to show compassion to you. This is so important. If you are not impressed by Jesus' greatness, you will likely be impressed by your own. And when you are impressed by your own greatness, you will not feel much compassion for others. So, look at Jesus!

First, think about His character.

There are so many reasons to love Jesus, so just pick one and set your heart on it like a bulldog with a bone. You might consider His relationship to God the Father. He is the beloved Son (Col. 1:13). You can think about His relationship to the universe. He is the one who designed it and created it and sustains it (Col. 1:15–16). You can focus on His relationship to the church. He is the head of the church—what's more, He's the reason the church exists (Col. 1:18). He is fully God and fully man (Col. 1:19). He's the one who's brought peace between believers and God and He did it through His death on the cross (Col. 1:20).

Ask God to help you to see Jesus in your Bible reading. When you study a passage, ask yourself what is in the passage that tells you about Jesus and gives you reason to love Him. Study the Gospels over and over. You know that Jesus reveals God, so as you study the Gospels, keep asking yourself what Jesus is teaching you about what God is like—especially what Jesus teaches you about God's attributes of lovingkindness, mercy, and compassion. Look for Jesus in your pastor's sermons. While you are in public worship, ask God to show you why you should love Jesus more as a result of what the pastor says. Another simple thing you might do to fill your heart with the love of Christ is to sing Christ-centered songs. Even if you don't feel like singing right away, begin singing songs that remind you of who Christ is, and sing them until your heart begins to heat up.

Second, think about your salvation.

You grow in your concern for others as you grow in your assurance of God's concern for you. If you are a Christian, God has been very good to you. But simply because you're a Christian doesn't mean you always appreciate how good He's been. You may need to work on enjoying the blessings that God has provided through Christ in your salvation. Just know that, when you do, you are actually working on becoming more compassionate as well.

If you don't trust that God is for you (see Rom. 8:31), it will be difficult for you to pour yourself out for others. It is hard to look out for the good of other people when you feel like you have to be looking out for your own. One reason you may be overly concerned with your own interests is because you are not enjoying all that Scripture says about God's interest in you. When you are convinced that God is for you because of what Jesus did, it enables you to be available for other people. After all, you cannot look out for your good better than God can, and God could not be more committed to your long-term good than He already is. Knowing that the Creator and Sustainer of the Universe is working all things together for your good gives you strength to focus on spending your energies working for other people's good instead of your own.

I live in an area where there are many beggars. One thing I have noticed about beggars is that they aren't usually very compassionate. Why? They are usually so focused on their own lack of resources that they don't believe they have anything to give to others. The same is true spiritually. If you feel like God hasn't given you much in salvation, you won't have much motivation to be compassionate. You will be so focused on what you *don't* have that you will convince yourself it is unreasonable for anyone to expect you to be concerned about others. It is when you begin to become amazed with the fact that you really do have every spiritual blessing in Christ, and that God has been overwhelmingly generous to you, that you begin to be motivated to be generous to others.

Getting to know how good God has been to you will take some effort. But you will probably be surprised by how meditating on these profound and mysterious truths can help you in some very practical ways. Take, for example, what the Bible teaches about God the Son and the incarnation. This is mysterious. I can sometimes think about the incarnation for only a few moments because it seems so complex. But this is the very truth that Paul brings up to help us to understand how to have unity in the church (see Phil. 2:4). The church's union with Christ is another truth that is very deep. Even Paul says, "This mystery is profound" (Eph. 5:32). Yet this is the very doctrine that he utilizes to enable us to better understand the way a husband should care for his wife. If you avoid thinking about truths just because they seem a little too difficult to understand at first, you may be avoiding the very thing that will help you most in your attitudes toward people.

The Cost of Compassion

Think of a compassionate lifestyle as being like a house: it requires a strong theological foundation.

It requires this strong theological foundation because compassion is not a gimmick. It's not a method to get people to like you or to accomplish some other end. It is not simply learning to nod your head and say, "Hmm," at the appropriate times. It doesn't take too much theology to do that. Biblical compassion involves sacrificing yourself for the glory of God and the good of others. True compassion involves deliberately choosing to enter into another person's pain. It is bearing an actual burden that is not your own. It is worshiping God by denying yourself in real life, and it takes a whole lot of theological understanding to do that.

It is actually pretty tempting to minimize the importance of compassionate concern for people, because compassionate concern is costly. It is easy to live the Christian life fueled by the same self-interest that energized us before we were converted. People sometimes pursue knowledge of the Bible for the same reasons they use to pursue knowledge in other realms—to appear smart, for example, or to get ahead. Knowing the right biblical answer can feed the same pride as knowing the right answer about anything else. You don't have to give up much to be an answer man, but there is a great deal you will have to give up if you really want to feel deeply and express that feeling to people.

The first thing you will have to give up is an obsessive concern with your own good.

You and I come into this world with a whole lot of concern for what's happening to us and with comparatively little concern for what's happening to others. If you have any doubts about that, just spend some time on a playground. You were focusing on yourself from day one, and you began developing thought and habit patterns from that point on that focused on yourself and your own interests. While you may have become a little better, I suppose, at covering up your self-interest as you grew older, it probably was primarily because covering up your self-interest made it possible for you to pursue your own interests with less resistance. Over time, this passionate pursuit of self becomes a self-centered lifestyle. And the point is that, if you don't deliberately turn from that self-centered lifestyle, it will cause you great difficulties in developing compassionate relationships.

You will never *feel* for other people until you *see* other people, and you will never see them until you are *interested* in them. And you will never become very interested in them until you become a little less interested in yourself. The problem most of us have is that we are too interested in ourselves to have much interest left for others. And even when we are interested in others, it is often only because they are interesting (or have something of interest) to us. If you and I are going to learn to show compassion, we must learn to be interested in people not because they are interesting in and of themselves but because we love them. When we begin to value and love people with the same intensity and fervor with which we love ourselves (see Mark 12:31; Rom. 12:10; Phil. 2:3–4), compassion is sure to follow. Compassion always follows interest.

One of the reasons we aren't as interested in others as we should be is because we have set ourselves at the center of our own little world. But we are really not the center of the world. God is. And He is up to something much bigger than simply taking care of us or exalting us. Yes, God is interested in us. But He's also interested in more than just us. When you find yourself struggling to be interested in people, step back and consider God's interest in them. That other person, the one you don't even notice, is the subject of God's intense interest. And what matters most is not your opinion of that person, but God's. What interests Him should interest you.

You know that God is interested in uninteresting people, because He created them. If the people you are struggling to feel compassion for are unbelievers, you must remember that they are God's creatures. What is more, they are made in His image. Don't think that you are so important that you can look down on your fellow man. The fact that others are made in God's image gives you a common bond with them, and it gives them great dignity.[9] While you might not think much of a particular person, God thought enough of her to give her the tremendous honor of bearing the beauty of His image. Whether or not she appreciates that, you should, as a Christian. And while you might be tempted to consider a particular person as not worth a moment of your time, the fact that he or she is a living human being who will live forever in either heaven or hell should cause you to think otherwise.

When you consider fellow believers, your reasons to show great concern and interest only multiply. How concerned is God with their good? You can look all the way back to before the beginning of the world and see Him planning their adoption. You can look in the Gospels and see Him accomplishing their salvation. You can look to what the Scriptures tell you about the end of time and you will see only the beginnings of His grace being poured upon them in their glorification.

How can you fail to be interested in people when God is this interested in them? What is more, how can you fail to be interested in them when, time and time again, God commands you to be interested in them?[10] When we are not interested in people, we are acting as if we were more important than God—so important that we don't have to submit to His will for our lives.

9. "Yet the great part of people are most unworthy to be helped if they be judged by their own merit. But here Scripture helps in the best way when it teaches that we are not to consider that men merit of themselves but to look upon the image of God in all men, to which we owe all honor and love. . . . There is but one way in which to achieve what is not merely difficult but utterly against human nature, to love those who hate us, to repay their evil deeds with benefits, to return blessings for reproaches. It is that we remember not to consider men's evil intention but to look upon the image of God in them, which cancels and effaces their transgressions, and with its beauty and dignity allures us to love and embrace them" (John Calvin, *Institutes of the Christian Religion* [Philadelphia: The Westminster Press, 1960], 1:696).

10. "Love one another with brotherly affection. Outdo one another in showing honor" (Rom. 12:10). "Let each of you look not only to his own interests, but also to the interests of others" (Phil. 2:4). "Let each of us please his neighbor for his good, to build him up" (Rom. 15:2).

I remember once talking to a leader who told me that he didn't really like people. The problem wasn't with people; it was with that leader. Somehow he had never learned to look at people the way God does. If you have a hard time valuing another believer, you might try to picture Christ dying on the cross for him. Then imagine yourself standing beside Christ dying on the cross for someone you couldn't care less about. How can you not love and care deeply for someone whom your Savior obviously cares so deeply about?

To feel correctly for people, you must think correctly about them. This means rejecting thoughts that diminish others, dismiss others, or degrade them, and putting on thoughts that correspond to their relationship with God. If they are unbelievers, you should think about the fact that they are currently enemies of God and, apart from repentance, will someday experience the wrath of God. Think about the consequences of their sin! Sin makes life here on earth worse, but more than that, the sin of those whom you have little or no compassion toward is dragging them toward an eternal hell. How can you not feel for someone who is facing that?

And if the person you are considering is a believer, there are many other biblically based thoughts upon which you can reflect. You might start to notice the way that Paul describes Christians in his various letters. Take 1 Corinthians as just one example of many. He doesn't begin, "Dear Corinthians, you are a group of rotten sinners, with all kinds of problems that really make me not even want to speak to you, but as an apostle of Christ I am supposed to be concerned about your sorry little souls, so here goes." Instead Paul writes,

> To the church of God that is in Corinth, to those sanctified in Christ Jesus, called to be saints together with all those who in every place call upon the name of our Lord Jesus Christ, both their Lord and ours: Grace to you and peace from God our Father and the Lord Jesus Christ. I give thanks to my God always for you because of the grace of God that was given you in Christ Jesus. (1 Cor. 1:2–4)

When you are struggling to feel compassion for a fellow believer, it is good to follow Paul's example and remember that the believer is more than a problem (or set of problems) to be dealt with; rather, he is a person who matters to—and is valued by—God.

One thing you might do if you don't feel deeply concerned about someone is to think about—imagine—what it would look like for you to be as interested in his good as God is (after all, compassion is an attribute of God that we are intended to imitate), and then act like that! Probably the most obvious and practical step you can take in this direction is to ask him questions and then listen attentively to his answers.[11] How can you say that you feel compassion for someone if you are unwilling to spend much time listening to her? Think of her heart as being filled with treasures, and then try to draw those treasures out (see Prov. 20:5). This means asking questions about what is happening in her life and how she feels about it. When you ask questions, work at being a patient listener. Listening involves a bit of personal sacrifice because it means you have to keep your mouth shut. But it is amazing what you can learn about a person when you stop talking and start hearing what he actually has to say about what is going on in his life. In fact, being a good listener can help you to communicate (and pursue) compassion even when you don't feel all that compassionate, in the same way that showing love communicates love even when one does not feel love (as for an enemy).

If you struggle with being concerned for others' interests, you might consider how you show concern for your own. After all, the second greatest commandment is to "love your neighbor as [with the same level of intensity as] you love yourself" (see Mark 12:31). When you find your mind repeatedly reviewing something that has happened to you, you might use that as an opportunity to learn how to be interested in others. Take hold of your thoughts and start thinking about someone else—what she

11. "Listen carefully to my speech, and let this be your way of consolation" (Job 21:2 NASB).

is experiencing—the way you were just thinking about yourself. Try to turn self-interest on its head and practice looking from every angle at what others are going through, the way you might look at what is happening to you. Take the way in which you show compassion to yourself as a model for the way you should show compassion for others.

When we talk about turning your attention from yourself to others like this, we really are talking about self-denial. Self-denial is not a slogan. It is a lifestyle. As B. B. Warfield explains,

> Self-sacrifice means not indifference to our times and our fellows; it means absorption in them. It means a forgetfulness of self in others. It means entering into every man's hopes and fears, longings and despairs, it means many-sidedness of spirit, multiform activity, multiplicity of sympathies. . . . It means not that we should live one life but a thousand lives, binding ourselves to a thousand souls by the filaments of so loving a sympathy that their lives become ours.[12]

We bind ourselves to others in the way Warfield describes because God has already bound us to them. We are one body, and it is important that we live and even feel like it (see 1 Cor. 12:26)!

The second thing you may have to give up in order to become more compassionate is your sense of superiority.

If you are going to feel correctly about others, you have to think correctly about yourself. Unfortunately, it is often very difficult to think correctly about yourself when you are trying to help someone else. When someone has a problem, you may be tempted to use what's happening to him as an excuse for feeling better about yourself. We are so intent on exalting ourselves over others that we will even use their sin to do so. How sad! Unfortunately, this becomes especially tempting when other people are struggling with different sins than you are. When

12. Warfield, *The Person and Work of Christ*, 574.

whatever is tempting them isn't a temptation for you, you can easily start thinking of yourself as being a little better than they are. And, if you are thinking like that, you are setting yourself up for a big fall—because, though you may be a different kind of sinner than they are, you are still a sinner.[13]

This passion for self-exaltation is part of what makes genuine compassion such a rare thing. There is a direct relationship between humility and compassion, and between pride and a lack of it. Thoughts and feelings of self-importance based on self-ignorance are a major hindrance to compassionate relationships. So mark it down. Apart from Christ, we are *nothing* spiritually. Imagine standing in a cemetery, surrounded by hundreds of gravestones, and shouting, "Look at me—I am so much better than you! I am alive!" No—physical life is a gift. So is spiritual life. Instead of being proud when you are around unbelievers, you should be overwhelmed with gratitude for God's grace. And, really, the same is true when you are with those who know Christ. If you have moved ahead spiritually or know more than they do, it is only because of help you have received from Christ. Every spiritual gift is a result of grace. How can anyone become proud of himself for that (1 Cor. 4:7)? If you have more gifts than someone else, it is only because you have been shown more mercy (see Rom. 12:3), which means that you, of everyone, have the most reason to be humble because you have received more grace.

If you are going to *feel compassion* for others, you need to *show no compassion* toward pride. When someone comes to you with a problem, you can assume that pride is going to come as well. Pride often uses occasions to show compassion as opportunities to promote itself instead. Suppose there is a needy person who is asking for your help. (Or maybe she is not asking for your help, but you think she really should.) If God in His grace has given you the wisdom

---

13. "For, such is the blindness with which we all rush into self-love that each one of us seems to himself to have just cause to be proud of himself and to despise all others in comparison" (Calvin, *Institutes*, 1:693).

you need to help such a troubled person, give thanks to Him and use your gifts to serve her. But watch out that you don't start taking yourself too seriously. If you have the answer that someone else needs, it is very tempting to start believing that *you* are the answer she needs. This is very dangerous because, once you start thinking of yourself as the Messiah, you stop acting very much like Him.

You might think it would be easy to spot this kind of proud heart. And it usually is—in *others*. It is much more difficult to see pride in yourself. Proud people usually don't think they are proud people. The first thing pride does is to poke your spiritual eyes out so that you are blind to it. That's why it is so important to consider the way you relate to others. People who are too hard on others are always too soft on themselves. Proud hearts always lead to cold hearts. The more you look up to yourself, the more you will look down on people.[14] If you are having trouble feeling compassion for people, you can be sure it is because you are too busy feeling impressed by yourself.

One way you can begin to fight this war on pride is by seeing other people's problems as your opportunities. Their problems are opportunities for you to do something even more important than giving them the answer they need. Their problems are opportunities for you to pursue the humility you need. Before you begin to look for a solution to somebody else's problem, slow down and make sure that you intentionally deal with your most significant problem, and that is pride. Commit yourself to doing something bigger than just saying the right thing. Commit yourself to feeling the right way for the person who needs your help.

Practical Steps toward Showing Compassion

1. Learn to treat other people like people instead of like projects.

It is not important how the mechanic feels about your car when he goes to fix it. But someone who comes to you with a

14. See, as one example, Luke 18:9: "He also told this parable to some who trusted in themselves that they were righteous, and treated others with contempt."

problem is not just a vehicle! He is a person made in the image of God, so it is very important how you feel about him. People mattered to Jesus, and they should matter to you.

One way to make it clear to people that they matter to you is by being approachable. If you think of yourself as too important to really listen to people who are hurting, you are thinking way too highly of yourself. Imagine if God did this with us! "Sorry, but I am too busy with My own agenda to deal with you right now—maybe I'll get back to you later when My schedule is clear." How good that He doesn't have such an attitude toward us! Treat other people with respect by relating to them the way you would want them to relate to you if you were in their shoes (see Matt. 7:12). Work hard at focusing on them.

You are busy, I understand! So was Jesus. When someone comes to you with a problem, that person is often seeking (if not even demanding) a great deal of your time. This is one reason why people whom the world considers important—and even Christians who consider themselves more important than they should—often struggle so much with showing compassion. Compassion takes time. It doesn't flourish when you are multitasking.

Compassion requires that you trust God enough to slow down and be as present with the person you are speaking to as if she were the only one in the room with you (whether she actually is or not). If you have overwhelming demands on your time that make it difficult for you to do this at the particular moment she comes to you with her problem, don't pretend otherwise. Instead, look at her and tell her that you do care about her and really want to be able to listen to what is going on in her life but have something that is pressing and needs to be taken care of quickly, making sure as you tell her this that you offer her an alternative time to sit down and talk. At the same time, however, be careful not to be too quick to use busyness as an excuse for not caring for people—especially for those who have immediate and pressing needs. When you find yourself beginning to allow projects that you have to finish to keep you from focusing on people, remind yourself of your own helplessness. Instead of allowing what you have to get done to distract you from the person you are ministering to, go to God in prayer. Tell Him that you are anxious and are absolutely dependent on His help to accomplish what you need to accomplish. Trust Him to help you make a wise decision about how to show compassion. Focus on the person who needs your help in that moment, even if you have to ask her to meet and speak at a different time. In this way your feeling of busyness can actually lead you toward compassion because it forces you to realize that you, too, are needy. After all, you are asking God for help at the very moment the other person is asking for your help.

2. Don't speak to those you are trying to help as if they don't know anything about what they are going through.

It's easy to treat someone who has questions as if he has never thought about the answers to the problems he is facing. This comes across as arrogance. Pride will tempt you to relate to others in ways that demean and diminish them. You must guard against having a dismissive attitude that quickly brushes aside the reasoning of others or minimizes the pain they might be going through. We aren't usually very gentle with people who we think aren't very smart. Humility demands that, when you speak to someone, you acknowledge that he may have already done or considered doing some of what you are suggesting. Though he may need your help, you must be careful not to think of him or treat him as if he were completely helpless. This is especially true if he is a Christian! After all, if he is a believer, he has a Bible and the Holy Spirit, just like you. When you think with this kind of humble respect about the people you are helping, you will begin to speak to them in compassionate ways. When you remember that the person you are speaking to is a thinking human being—and, if a Christian, someone who is being taught and trained by God—it changes the way that you approach him with suggested solutions to his problems. Instead of rushing in as a "know it all," you will ask for his perspective and listen[15] to what he thinks may be the solution to the problem being faced. You will verbally acknowledge that he may have already been thinking about this issue—since, after all, it is his life. You might admit that you may be telling him things he has already considered. You will assure him that the reason you are sharing your advice is not because you believe you are smarter or wiser or more spiritually mature than he is, but instead because you love him and want to be of any help you can.

3. Think about more than just what you are going to say to people who are hurting—think about to whom you are saying it.

It is strange and often offensive to anyone who has ever been hurt deeply to be treated as if all he needed was correct information. Hurting people need that, certainly, but they also need you—all of you (your heart as well as your intellect)! It is particularly common for people who are hurting deeply to feel as if others don't understand what they are going through. They often believe that they haven't truly been heard. And if they feel that they haven't been heard, they are going to be tempted not to hear what is being said to them. Therefore you must go to great lengths to make sure that the people you are speaking with know that you really want to understand how they are experiencing what's happening to them. This usually means that you will have to listen patiently to a lot of words at first, without doing a whole lot of interrupting or correcting or giving answers. It is sometimes helpful to say things like, "I am hearing you say that. . . . Am I hearing you correctly?" Or, "I can hardly imagine how difficult

15. Proverbs 18:2, 13, 17.

33

it was for you to go through something like this. . . . How did that make you feel?" You may feel as if you aren't doing anything when you sit there and listen like this, but if you are showing concern for the people you are speaking to, you are doing something very important and are making it much easier for them to listen when you do finally begin to share biblical solutions with them.

You need to have a servant's mindset with your words. As you speak, you are not just getting the truth out and dumping that truth on people; rather, you are thinking about the occasion and about what that person needs. You are asking yourself, "What is going on in this person's life?"; "What is she struggling with?"; "What does he understand? What does he need to understand?"; and, "How can I, through my words at this moment, serve this person for the glory of Christ?"

4. Make sure you are speaking words that are biblically true in a manner that is biblically appropriate.

Speaking in compassionate ways will require putting off certain wrong ways of communicating with others. For example, in Ephesians 4:31, Paul tells us to "Let . . . clamor . . . be put away from [us]." The word *clamor* here basically means yelling, and you are going to have to put that off in order to treat people compassionately.

Now, let me explain exactly what this means, because obviously God doesn't have a problem with volume. The world is a pretty loud place, and I am sure He is not wearing earmuffs. He tells us throughout the Psalms that we are to shout for joy. There are times when it is totally appropriate to be loud, when it would be wrong not to. The yelling that He is talking about putting off is more than just speaking up. It is the kind of speech that is motivated by anger. It is not shouting encouragement at your son's basketball game; it's screaming at him on the ride home for not playing hard enough.

It may be helpful to understand why people yell and, especially, why certain kinds of yelling aren't appropriate for someone who believes the gospel and wants to show compassion.

One reason that people yell is habit. This is a superficial
reason, of course, and it doesn't quite get to the heart of it,
but at the same time there's no question that some people
feel much more comfortable with yelling because they grew
up in families where shouting at others was perfectly normal.
This is part of the reasoning Paul uses when he says we have
to put it off. Even though we are believers, some of us may
have developed a habitual pattern of yelling at others. This
pattern may have come from our days as unbelievers living
in an unbelieving culture, but now that we are believers, we
need to step up and apply what we believe—all the way to
our tone of speech.

Another reason people yell is to punish or abuse. Instead of
using their fists, some use their mouths. Their words become
weapons, which they use to humiliate others. This usually occurs
when they are angry. Their anger produces extra energy that they
use to attack and destroy others. The people they are speaking
to become their verbal punching bags.

Probably the ultimate reason people yell at others is
because they don't trust God. In particular, there are two
truths about God that people deny when they are screaming
at others.

It may be, first, that the person who is yelling doesn't
trust *that God is in control of the situation* she finds herself in.
Think about it. Why do you yell? It is because your emotions
are worked up. You don't usually scream at random. And why
are your emotions worked up? It is often because you are afraid
that the situation is getting out of control. You yell because
you want to try to bring the situation back under your control.
But is the situation really out of control? Of course it is not.
God is in absolute control! When you are confident of God's
control, you may speak sternly, as I imagine Jesus did to the

storm on the Sea of Galilee, but you won't be freaking out like the disciples were on the boat.

Or, second, it may be that the person who is yelling doesn't trust *that God is for him in the situation* he finds himself in. Yelling is often a means of manipulating others into to giving us what we want. We have an agenda. The other person is making it difficult for us to accomplish our agenda. So we take matters into our own hands (or, as one might say, into our own voice) and we use our voice to try to force the other person to do what we desire.

What should we do instead? We should trust that God knows what is best for us, that He is absolutely committed to accomplishing our good, and that, in the moment we find ourselves in, He is actually doing just that. When we believe that God is totally committed to our ultimate good, it frees us up from trying to force the person who seems to be getting in our way into doing what we think is best for us, and it allows us to be focused on exactly what we should be focused on—glorifying God by submitting to His will and seeking the best for others.

How crazy would I be if I thought I could actually pursue my own good better than the almighty Creator and Sustainer of the Universe can? How crazy would I be if I thought I actually knew what was good for me better than He does? And since He has promised that He is for me (see Rom. 8:31), I don't need to worry about using my words for myself. I can commit myself, instead, to using my words for Him.

The fact that we are believers should impact the way we communicate, all the way down to the tone of voice we use with others when they are not doing what we want them to. It doesn't mean that we stop taking sin seriously or that we don't ever speak sternly or strongly. But believing that God is in control, and that He is for us because of the work of Jesus Christ, should keep us from speaking to others out of fear, shame, or manipulation. It should motivate us to start working on putting off old habits—such as clamor.

5. Refuse to use your speech to tear others down.

Becoming compassionate will require you to put off the kind of speech described in James 4:11. James writes, "Do not speak evil against one another, brothers." We speak evil against others when we speak words that are intended to hurt rather than to help. More specifically, we speak evil against others when we speak words that are produced by pride rather than humility. We know this because James goes on to explain what it means to speak against others by saying,

> He who speaks against a brother, or *judges his brother*, speaks evil against the law and judges the law. But if you judge the law, you are not a doer of the law but a judge. There is only one lawgiver and judge, he who is able to save and to destroy. But who are you to judge your neighbor? (James 4:11–12)

When James talks about not speaking against others and not judging others, he's not talking about lovingly dealing with someone's sin. He's not talking about humbly going to someone and dealing with an issue. Instead he's talking about selfish speech. He is talking about speech that has one purpose—to make you look good and to make others look bad. He is talking about speech that is motivated by selfishness, not selflessness, and is characterized by pride rather than humility.

What exactly does this kind of speech look like? There are almost too many examples to mention. It is when we say things that we know aren't true about other people just because we want to make them look bad. It is when we say things about others without knowing whether they're true or not, just because we enjoy looking like we know something important. It is when we exaggerate a person's faults. It is when we speak in hypercritical ways. It is when we speak as if we, rather than God, were the final standard of what is right and wrong.

The way you speak to others reveals a great deal about what is happening in your heart (see Luke 6:45). As you pursue humble compassion, it is important that you think about how you are speaking to others and whether or not your words are motivated by a desire to make yourself look good by tearing others down.

To evaluate your speech, you might ask yourself the following kinds of questions:

- Am I saying something about someone else that isn't true or helpful?
- Am I speaking too quickly? Are my words thoughtful?
- Could I describe my words as soft? This doesn't mean that they are not direct or not addressing sin, but as I address those issues, am I doing so in a way that could be described as gentle?
- Am I being sneaky with my speech? Am I saying something in a certain way in order to manipulate the situation in my favor? Am I trying to appear as if I am doing one thing when I have a larger goal in the back of my mind that is the exact opposite?
- Am I making it easier for the person to whom I am talking to argue with me?
- Am I speaking because my feelings have been hurt, or am I looking out for the other person's good?
- Does the way I am talking sound like a person who is slow to become angry? Am I picking up on every mistake the person is making and going after it with my words, or am I quick to overlook an offense?

6. Practice speaking in loving, gracious, and gentle ways.

One of the ways to pursue compassion is to specifically work on speaking in ways that build others up. The Bible speaks about a wholesome kind of talk—that is, talk that is not corrupting (Eph. 4:29). There is a kind of speech that makes relationships sick and there is a kind of speech that makes relationships healthy. "There is one whose rash words are like sword thrusts, but the tongue of the wise brings healing" (Prov. 12:18).

What does health-producing speech look like, exactly? My father, Wayne Mack, is a biblical counselor. One of the things I have always appreciated about him is that he works hard at taking biblical principles and applying them to the nitty-gritty issues of life. Here are some possible real-life examples he gives of the difference between speech that sickens and speech that gives life:

Uncompassionate: Stop ordering me around. You are so bossy. Who do you think you are, anyway?

Compassionate: When you would like me to do something, I would appreciate it if you would ask me to do it rather than demanding that I do it.

Uncompassionate: Don't you talk to me like that. If you ever do, I guarantee I will make sure you never do it again.

Compassionate: The tone of voice you are using with me is tempting me to become frightened or angry or to respond in a sinful way.

Uncompassionate: You'd better listen to me or you will be sorry.

Compassionate: Right now I am getting the impression that you aren't very interested in what I am saying. Is that true? Would there be a better time for me to talk to you about this?

Uncompassionate: It is obvious you are bitter. Why can't you see it? You need to look me right in the eye and ask my forgiveness, because I know that you are angry even if you don't know you are.

Compassionate: I have been getting the sense that you are really disappointed with me about some things. Am I right? What exactly have I been doing that has been making it difficult for you? Is it possible that there's some anger in your heart toward me right now?

Uncompassionate: I will tell you one thing. If you won't do it, I will find someone who will.

Compassionate: Please help me to understand why you don't want to do what I have asked you to do.

Uncompassionate: That's a stupid idea. What you are suggesting is ridiculous. Why would you ever think it would work?

Compassionate: Let me make sure I understand what you are saying and why you think that way.

Uncompassionate: You are doing it all wrong! The way you are doing it doesn't make sense. Let me tell you a better way to do it!

Compassionate: I know you like the way you are doing it, and it's okay with me if you want to do it that way. Would you mind, though, if I suggest another way of doing it that might save a little energy?

Uncompassionate: You are so funny when you get mad. I really get a kick out of the way you get red in the face and glare at me when you get mad. It's so funny to see you acting in the childish ways you do. Your pouting and sulking remind me of what some of our children used to do when they didn't get their way, back when they were babies.

Compassionate: You seem upset. Are you? What is it I have done or said that displeases you? What could I have done differently that would have been less problematic for you?[16]

Unfortunately, sometimes we Christians are so wrapped up in ourselves that we don't think about how the way we are speaking affects the people facing us. Perhaps we are speaking the truth, but we are speaking the truth in a selfish way because we are not concerned about the person we are speaking the truth to.

16. Wayne A. Mack, "Communication in Marriage and Family" (lecture, Lynwood Baptist Church, Lynwoodridge, South Africa, February 15, 2015).

We need to work on learning the language of compassion. As you practice using compassionate words to communicate to others, pray that God will help you to believe and truly feel what you are saying. As you speak to others using compassionate speech instead of uncompassionate words, you will often find God producing in you feelings of concern for others that you haven't felt before.

7. Take time to pray with people who are hurting.

Obvious? Not always—especially not for proud people. All too often, those who are attempting to help struggling people will jump in and try to fix the problem on their own without depending on God. If anything, maybe they will utter a quick prayer but then get right into the issue. What about just slowing down with the person you are ministering to, getting on your knees together, and saying something like, "God, we are confused about how to deal with this problem and we know it would be very easy to make things worse, so we are just coming before You crying out that You would give us the ability to know what to do next"?

8. Make sure you are willing to learn from people who are suffering.

If you are helping someone who is in the middle of difficult circumstances, it is easy to begin thinking of yourself as the problem solver and of the other person as the problem. Life is more complex than that. What if God is using the other person's struggles not only to bring him to greater maturity, but to do the same for you? What if what's happening to him is a moment for you to learn something? Actually, there's really no "what if" about it. When you begin seeing the person to whom you are ministering as someone who has something to teach you, you will generally stop seeing yourself as someone who is superior. This will open the door so that compassion can flow into and out of your heart more freely.

9. Make it clear to the people to whom you are ministering that you love them and that God does, too.

The more pain adds up, the more questions multiply. The person whom you are helping needs something bigger than simply an answer to her immediate concerns. She needs hope! She needs assurance! One means that God uses to give other people hope is through loving relationships. Something significant happens when you know that someone has your best interests at heart.

You may think it is obvious that you care for the other person. After all, you are there speaking to her. But it is not always that simple. When someone is hurting deeply, she is usually also feeling very insecure. This is why the compassionate person doesn't only tell such a person what to do, but also tells her that he loves her. At first this may seem awkward for you. But try this. Look at the person you are talking to and say, "I want you to know that I really appreciate you and love you." That person can't see into your heart and doesn't know what's there if you don't say it. Now, I understand that telling people outside your family that you love them may feel strange to you, but you must get over that. This is part of pursuing humility in real life.

Don't just tell them that you love them, however. Do whatever you can to help them become convinced of God's great love for them as well. Compassion requires you to help them appreciate this truth! The greatest problem that people can have is not knowing God's love for them. The greatest solution that you can offer them is helping them to discover and enjoy that love. You want to help them move past simply knowing God as an idea or a fact and instead to delight in God as a *person*. Math teachers don't need to show much concern for their students, because they are teaching them a subject, but you are doing something for people that is much bigger than that. You are introducing them to a person, *the* Person, and you want to make sure you represent Him well!

10. Surround yourself with people who are compassionate.

Our family once took a trip to visit friends in Germany. I will always remember our time there, because I have never been shown hospitality like that. Their unselfish concern for us exposed how selfish I had been in the way I reached out to others who had visited me. It motivated me to work harder on expressing concern for others and gave me a pattern to follow in how to do that. I had heard sermons on hospitality, and I had even preached sermons on hospitality, but seeing hospitality helped me to take those principles and apply them more specifically to my life.

I am convinced that the same is true with compassion. God designed us to learn from, and be influenced by, the way people live. This is why, when Paul discipled people, he not only provided verbal and written instruction but also challenged people to take note of his example. It is interesting to read his letters and notice how many times he calls on others to imitate him (1 Cor. 4:16, 11:1; Phil. 3:17; 1 Thess. 1:6; 2 Thess. 3:7). Paul went about training people this way because he knew that, for us to change, we need not only to hear instruction but also to see how that instruction is applied in real life. If you are going to become more compassionate, it is good to read about compassion and to listen to sermons about love. But it is also vital to spend time with people who are living a compassionate lifestyle. Watch them. Listen to the way they communicate. Don't defend yourself and make excuses for yourself when those people are less selfish than you are. Instead, allow yourself to be challenged by them, and even deliberately attempt to imitate them.

The book of Proverbs warns us not to make a friendship with a man given to anger, lest we learn his ways (Prov. 22:24–25). I am convinced that we can take this proverb and flip it on its head. We should make friendships with people who are given to compassion so that we can learn their ways!

11. Think about the pressing needs of those around you and make sacrifices to meet them, expecting nothing in return.

True compassion produces merciful acts, and merciful acts often produce true compassion. With all that's been said about how compassion involves feelings, it is important to stress that true compassion doesn't usually end with feelings, and it may not even start there. We often don't feel what we should toward others because we are not doing what we should in our relationship with them. When we begin considering their interests above our own, working on getting to know them, spending time with them, listening to them, seeing what is happening in their lives, and making sacrifices to help them succeed in their relationship with Christ, those acts of obedience will provide the soil in which feelings of compassion can grow.

I am pastor of an inner-city church in South Africa. Our church is made up of all different kinds of cultures and social backgrounds. This mix of classes can make compassionate relationships difficult initially. Each group has stereotypes of the other groups in mind, which can make feeling empathy for them more challenging. It can be hard for those from poorer backgrounds, for example, to believe that those who are financially well off have any real problems at all, and it can certainly be difficult for those who have been blessed with opportunities and resources to understand how challenging life can be when someone lacks those same privileges. Initially both groups are tempted to feel suspicion, rather than compassion, toward one another, but I have found time after time that when believers, motivated by a desire to honor Christ, seek to obey the "one another" commands of Scripture and begin to do the hard work of caring for people who are different than they are, God breaks down those barriers and begins producing genuine compassion in their hearts for others.

It will take work to feel right. I guarantee it. And I wouldn't be surprised if you feel a little overwhelmed as you begin to think about making some of the changes you need to make in order to become a more compassionate person. Representing Jesus well is not going to be easy. Given how proud and selfish we are, and how many bad habits we have developed over the years, we can be certain that becoming more compassionate is going to require effort. But really, given the fact that we are representing Someone whose compassion for sinners like us took Him to the cross to die in our place, should we expect anything less?

Though the process of becoming more compassionate may be hard for you, I guarantee that it will also be good for you. God has packed the path toward compassion with His grace. You cannot take steps toward becoming more compassionate to others without also growing in your appreciation of God's great compassion to you. To show compassion you must know God's compassion, and, what's more, as you show compassion to others, God will reveal His compassion for you more and more.

Discussion Questions

1. What does it mean to be compassionate?

2. What does compassion have to do with the way you feel?

3. What are some reasons it is important to be compassionate?

4. What are some of the truths that 1 Peter 1:22-25 teaches us about the nature of biblical love?

5. What are some of the different ways that God emphasizes the importance of love?

6. Why is it vital to understand that passion for truth must produce compassion for people?

7. What can we learn from Paul and Jesus about the importance of showing compassion to people? What can we learn from them about relating to people?

8. What are some ways that people defend themselves when confronted about their lack of compassion? What are some reasons those defenses are inadequate?

9. What does it mean that a lack of compassion is a worship problem?

10. What is the connection between appreciating God's compassion for you and becoming more compassionate toward others?

11. How does Paul motivate believers to show compassionate, forgiving love in Ephesians 4:32-5:2?

12. What does Luke 7:47 teach us about the root of a problem with loving others?

13. Explain the following statement in your own words: "What you believe about your sinfulness is revealed best in the way you relate to others."

14. Why is looking to the character of God an even better motivation for showing compassion to others than simply looking to the needs of people?

15. What can we learn from 2 Corinthians 3:18 about the process of becoming a more compassionate person?

16. What are some different ways you can work on loving Jesus more? How will this help you to love others better?

17. How is a lack of compassion sometimes tied to a lack of faith?

18. What will you have to give up if you are going to become more compassionate?

19. What reasons do you have for showing compassion to an unbeliever? What are some reasons you have for being compassionate even to someone who you don't believe deserves it?

20. What are some of the reasons you have for being compassionate to a believer? When you are struggling to feel compassion for someone else, what are some of the biblically based thoughts you can think about that person which will motivate you to show compassion to him?

21. How can looking at the way you love yourself help you to learn how to show concern for others?

22. Why is it especially tempting to feel superior to someone else when he comes to you with a problem? Why are these feelings of superiority especially foolish?

23. What is the connection between pride and lack of compassion?

24. What does it mean to treat others like people and not like projects? How can you make it clear to others that they matter to you?

25. What can you do if you are very busy and someone is asking for your time and help? How can you show compassion to such a person in that moment?

26. Why is it important not to treat the people you are trying to help as if they were completely helpless? How will that help you to treat them with compassion? What are some of the dangers of acting as if someone were completely helpless when you go to show him compassion?

27. When people are hurting deeply, what are some particular needs they have beyond just receiving correct information?

28. How should the gospel impact even your tone of voice as you speak with others?

29. What are some ways in which people use their speech to tear others down? Why is this particularly tempting when people are hurting?

30. If you had to summarize in a sentence what wholesome speech looks like, what would you say?

31. Suggest some reasons why it is important to tell people who are hurting that you love them. Why is that sometimes difficult for us to do? What are some specific ways you can work on becoming better at expressing your compassion for others?

32. Whom do you know to be a particularly compassionate person? What can you learn from this person about what compassion looks like in real life? What are some of the things this person has done that have made a particular impression on your life? What could you do to follow in his or her footsteps?

33. What should you do if you are not feeling compassion toward someone else?

34. How can you be different as a result of what you have read in this booklet? How will you change? What are some of the truths from this booklet that you would most like to share with others?